Dr. Sadhasivam Narayanan

Certain Investigation on Improved PSO Algorithm for Workflow Scheduling in Cloud Computing Environments

Anchor Academic
Publishing

Narayanan, Sadhasivam: Certain Investigation on Improved PSO Algorithm for
Workflow Scheduling in Cloud Computing Environments, Hamburg, Anchor Academic
Publishing 2017

Buch-ISBN: 978-3-96067-192-3
PDF-eBook-ISBN: 978-3-96067-692-8
Druck/Herstellung: Anchor Academic Publishing, Hamburg, 2017

Bibliografische Information der Deutschen Nationalbibliothek:
Die Deutsche Nationalbibliothek verzeichnet diese Publikation in der Deutschen
Nationalbibliografie; detaillierte bibliografische Daten sind im Internet über
http://dnb.d-nb.de abrufbar.

Bibliographical Information of the German National Library:
The German National Library lists this publication in the German National Bibliography.
Detailed bibliographic data can be found at: http://dnb.d-nb.de

© Anchor Academic Publishing, Imprint der Diplomica Verlag GmbH
Hermannstal 119k, 22119 Hamburg
http://www.diplomica-verlag.de, Hamburg 2017
Printed in Germany

Dr. Sadhasivam Narayanan

Certain Investigation on Improved PSO Algorithm for Workflow Scheduling in Cloud Computing Environments

Anchor Academic
Publishing

Narayanan, Sadhasivam: Certain Investigation on Improved PSO Algorithm for Workflow Scheduling in Cloud Computing Environments, Hamburg, Anchor Academic Publishing 2017

Buch-ISBN: 978-3-96067-192-3
PDF-eBook-ISBN: 978-3-96067-692-8
Druck/Herstellung: Anchor Academic Publishing, Hamburg, 2017

Bibliografische Information der Deutschen Nationalbibliothek:
Die Deutsche Nationalbibliothek verzeichnet diese Publikation in der Deutschen Nationalbibliografie; detaillierte bibliografische Daten sind im Internet über http://dnb.d-nb.de abrufbar.

Bibliographical Information of the German National Library:
The German National Library lists this publication in the German National Bibliography. Detailed bibliographic data can be found at: http://dnb.d-nb.de

---

© Anchor Academic Publishing, Imprint der Diplomica Verlag GmbH
Hermannstal 119k, 22119 Hamburg
http://www.diplomica-verlag.de, Hamburg 2017
Printed in Germany

TABLE OF CONTENTS

CERTAIN INVESTIGATION ON IMPROVED PSO ALGORITHM

FOR WORKFLOW SCHEDULING IN CLOUD COMPUTING

ENVIRONMENTS

Dr. N. SADHASIVAM
Assistant Professor (Senior Grade),
Department of Computer Science and Engineering,
Bannari Amman Institute of Technology, Erode, India
E-mail: sadhasivamn82@gmail.com

ABSTRACT

Recent collaborative scientific experiments in domains such as molecular biology, neuro-science and high-energy physics have made if necessary to involve the management of distributed data sources. As a result, an analysis of their datasets is represented and structured as scientific workflows. In general, these kind of scientific workflows need to process a large amount of data and computationally intensive activities. To manage these scientific experiments, a scientific workflow management system is used by hiding the orchestration and integration details inherent while executing workflows on distributed resources provided by cloud service providers.

Cloud computing is a new prototype for enterprises that can effectively assist the execution of tasks. Task scheduling is a major constraint which greatly influences the performance of cloud computing environment. The cloud service providers and consumers have different objectives and requirements. For the moment, the load and availability of the resources vary dynamically with time. Therefore, in the cloud environment scheduling

1

resources is a complicated problem. Moreover, task scheduling algorithm is a method by which tasks are allocated or matched to data center resources.

All task scheduling problems in cloud computing environment come under the class of combinatorial optimization problems which decide searching for an optimal solution in a finite set of potential solutions. For a combinatorial optimization problem in bounded time exact algorithms always guarantee to find an optimal solution for every finite size instance. These kinds of problems are NP-Hard in nature. Moreover, for the large scale applications, exact algorithm needs unexpected computation time which leads to the increase in computational burden. However, absolutely perfect scheduling algorithm does not exist, because of conflicting scheduling objectives. Therefore, to overcome this constraint heuristic algorithms are proposed. In workflow scheduling problems, search space grows exponentially with the problem size. Heuristics optimization is search methods useful in local search to find good solutions quickly in a restricted area. The Heuristics optimization methods do not provide a suitable solution for scheduling problem.Researchers have shown good performance of metaheuristic algorithms in a wide range of complex problems.

In order to minimize the defined objective of task resource mapping, improved versions of Particle Swarm Optimization (PSO) is put in place to enhance scheduling performance with less computational burden. In the recent years, PSO has been successfully applied to solve different kinds of problems, ranging from multimodal and topological mathematical problems to aerospace and chemical engineering. It is famous for its easy realization and fast convergence, while suffering from the possibility of early convergence to local optimums. In the proposed Improved Particle Swarm Optimization (IPSO) algorithm, whenever early convergence occurs, the original particle swarm would be considered the worst positions an individual particle and worst positions global particle the whole swarm have experienced.

Keywords: Workflow Scheduling, Cloud Computing Environment, Scheduling Algorithm, Optimization, Metaheuristic Optimization, PSO, IPSO

2

1. Introduction

In the modern world, the scientific workflow applications in domains such as molecular biology, neuro-science and high-energy physics have to involve the management of distributed data sources. An analysis of the scientific applications datasets can be represented as a structure of scientific workflows. In general, these kind of scientific workflows need to process a large amount of data and computationally intensive activities. Scientific workflow Management Systems are used to o manage these scientific applications by hiding the inherent orchestration and integration details while executing workflows on distributed resources provided by cloud service providers (Talia 2013).

1.1 Cloud Computing

The word "cloud" comes from the terminology of those who built and sold client server applications, software and hardware used to draw a picture with the Personal Computer (PC) connected to a network and the network connected to a server. The cloud is a metaphor for delivery of hosted services over the internet. Technically, it is a computing paradigm in which tasks are assigned to a combination of connections, software and services accessed over a network. The network of servers and connections is collectively known as the cloud computing. Physically, the resource may sit on a bunch of servers at different data centres or even span across continents. Cloud computing is a computing platform that resides in a service provider's large data centre and is capable of dynamically providing servers the ability to address a wide range of needs of clients.

Computing at the scale of the cloud allows users to access supercomputer-level power. Instead of operating their own data centres, firms might rent computing power and storage capacity from a service provider, making them pay only for what they use, as they do with electricity or water. The paradigm of cloud computing has also been referred to as "utility computing," in which computing capacity is treated like any other metered utility service-one pays only for what one uses.

Users can reach into the cloud for resources as they need from anywhere at anytime. For this reason, cloud computing has also been described as "on-demand computing". It is provided as a service by another company and accessed over the Internet, usually in a

3

completely seamless way. Exactly where the hardware and software are located and how they all work do not matter to users. For the user it is just somewhere up in the nebulous "cloud" that the Internet represents.

Cloud computing was coined for what happens when applications and services are moved into the internet "cloud." Cloud computing is not something that suddenly appeared overnight; in some form it may be traced back to a time when computer systems remotely time-shared computing resources and applications. More currently though, cloud computing refers to the many different types of services and applications being delivered in the internet cloud. In many cases, the devices used to access these services and applications do not require any special applications.

Many companies are delivering services from the cloud. Some notable examples as of 2016 include the following:

Amazan has a private web services and allows users to upload and access music, videos, documents, and photos from Web-connected devices. The service also enables users to stream music to their devices and also provides different services. Google has a private cloud that it uses for delivering many different services to its users, including email access, document applications, text translations, maps, web analytics, and much more.

Microsoft has Microsoft Share point online service that allows content and business intelligence tools to be moved into the cloud, and Microsoft currently makes its office applications available in a cloud.

Salesforce.com runs its application set for its customers in a cloud, and its Force.com and Vmforce.com products provide developers with platforms to build customized cloud services.

1.2 Task Scheduling

Cloud computing is a nascent prototype for enterprises that can effectively assist in the execution of tasks. A scheduling algorithm for elastic processes is responsible for finding a workflow execution plan which makes sure that all workflows are carried out under the given constraints. These constraints could be defined in a Service Level Agreement (SLA). Based on this scheduling plan, the reasoner is able to allocate, lease,

4

and release cloud-based computational resources. Scheduling has to be done continuously for an unknown duration of time, across a system landscape including the business process landscape as well as cloud resources so that:

All SLAs defined for workflows are met.

- Resources are utilized in an efficient way, i.e. the costs for leasing Virtual Machines (VMs) over the reckoned time span should be optimized.
- Scheduling and reasoning need to be redone once the system landscape changes, as new workflow requests arrive or the predicted resource utilization of VMs does not apply.
- In addition, scheduling and reasoning are done at regular intervals. This interval can be set by a system administrator.

In order to find a scheduling, one can make use of the following constraints:

- Each backend VMs hosts exactly one service instance, i.e. it is not possible that different service types are instantiated at the same backend VMs.
- All VMs offer the same capabilities in terms of computational resources and costs.

Task scheduling is a major concern which greatly influences the performance of cloud computing environment. The cloud service providers and consumers have different objectives and requirements. For the moment, the load and availability of the resources vary dynamically with time. Therefore, in the cloud environment scheduling resources is a complicated problem. Moreover, task scheduling algorithm is a method by which tasks are allocated or matched to data center resources. However, absolutely perfect scheduling algorithms do not exist because of conflicting scheduling objectives (Pandey et al. 2010).

Workflow scheduling is the problem of mapping each task to appropriate resource and allowing the tasks to satisfy some performance criterion. A workflow consists of a sequence of concatenated (connected) steps. Workflow mainly focuses on with the automation of procedures and also in order to achieve the overall goal thereby files and data are passed between participants according to a defined set of rules. The workflow enables the structuring of applications in a directed acyclic graph form where each node

5

represents the task and edges represent the dependencies between the nodes of the applications.

A single workflow consists of a set of tasks and each task communicates with another task in the workflow. Workflows are supported by Workflow Management Systems (WMS). Workflow scheduling discovers resources and allocates tasks on suitable resources. Workflow scheduling plays a vital role in the workflow management. Proper scheduling of workflow can have an efficient impact on the performance of the system. However, for proper scheduling of workflows, various scheduling algorithms are used.

1.3 Task Scheduling Algorithms

A good scheduler applies a combination of scheduling algorithms or implements a suitable compromise according to the different applications. Depending on the algorithm applied, a problem can be solved in seconds, hours or even years. Algorithm efficiency is evaluated by the amount of time necessary to execute it. Task scheduling problem is the problem of matching tasks to different sets of resources. Scheduling problem can be classified into two types such as optimization problem and decision problem based on the objectives (Omara & Afara 2010).

Scheduling problems belong to a broad class of combinational optimization problem, aimed at finding an optimal matching of tasks to different sets of resources. A hierarchy of task scheduling algorithms (Pandey et al. 2010) is shown in Figure 1.1. In order to schedule the tasks efficiently and cost effectively, the schedulers have different policies that vary according to the objective functions. They minimize the total cost to execute, the total execution time and balance the load on resources used while meeting the deadline constraints of the application and so forth.

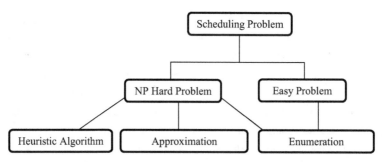

Figure 1.1 A hierarchy of task scheduling algorithms

1.4 Metaheuristic Optimization

Optimization is essentially everywhere, from engineering design to economics and from holiday planning to Internet routing. As money, resources and time are always limited, the optimal utility of these available resources is crucially important. Many engineering optimization problems are usually quite difficult to solve, and many applications have to deal with these complex problems. In these problems, search space grows exponentially with the problem size. Therefore, the traditional optimization methods do not provide a suitable solution for them. Hence, over the past few decades, many metaheuristic algorithms had been designed to solve such problems.

Researchers have shown good performance of metaheuristic algorithms in a wide range of complex problems such as scheduling, data clustering, image and video processing, tuning of neural networks, pattern recognition etc. Algorithms with stochastic components were often referred to as heuristic in the past, though the recent literature tends to refer to them as metaheuristics. It seems to be advisable to follow Glover's convention and call all modern nature-inspired algorithms metaheuristics (Glover 1986, Glover & Kochenberger 2003). Loosely speaking, heuristic means to find or to discover by trial and error. Here meta means beyond or higher level, and metaheuristics generally perform better than simple heuristics.

The word "metaheuristic" was coined by Fred Glover in his seminal paper (Glover 1986) and a metaheuristic can be considered as a "master strategy that guides and modifies other heuristics to produce solutions beyond those that are normally generated in a quest for local optimality" (Glover & Laguna 1997). In addition, all metaheuristic algorithms use a certain trade off of randomization and local search. Quality solutions to difficult optimization problems can be found in a reasonable amount of time, but there is no guarantee that optimal solutions can be reached. It is hoped that these algorithms work most of the time, but not all the time. Almost all metaheuristic algorithms tend to be suitable for global optimization. In this connection, it seems relevant to recall the excellent review that Voss (2001) given.

Two major components of any metaheuristic algorithms are: intensification and diversification or exploitation and exploration (Blum & Roli 2003). Diversification means to generate diverse solutions so as to explore the search space on a global scale, while intensification means to focus the search in a local region knowing that a current good solution is found in this region. A good balance between intensification and diversification should be found during the selection of the best solutions to improve the rate of algorithm convergence. The selection of the best ensures that solutions will converge to the optimum, while diversification via randomization allows the search to escape from local optima and at the same time, increases the diversity of solutions. A good combination of these two major components will usually ensure that global optimality is achievable.

1.5   Task to Resource Scheduling Paradigm

A workflow application is a graph $G=(V,E)$ that can be represented by a Directed Acyclic Graph (DAG), where V is the set of n tasks $\{T1, T2,......,Tn\}$ and E is a set of e edges, that represents the dependencies. Each $Ti \in V$, represents a task in the application and each edge (ei..........ej) $\in$ E represents a precedence constraint, such that the execution of $Tj \in V$ cannot be started before $Ti \in V$ finishes its execution. A task with no parent is known as an entry or root task and a task with no children is known as exit or last task.

Consider a set of compute resources PC = {1, ..., j} and a set of tasks T = {1, ...,
k}. The cost of computation of a task on a compute host is inversely proportional to the
time it takes for computation on that resource. Then, the time it takes for computation on
that resource is inversely proportional to the cost of computation of a task on a compute
host. Consider that the cost of unit data access $d_{i,j}$ from a resource i to a resource j is
known. The transfer cost can be calculated according to the bandwidth between the
resources.

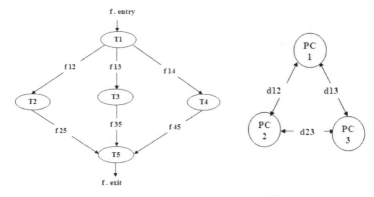

Figure 1.2 Sample workflow & compute resources (PC)

Figure 1.2 depicts the workflow structure with five tasks (Pandey et al. 2010),
which are represented as nodes. The dependencies among tasks are represented by arrows.
The entry task may have an input file (e. g. f.entry) and the exit task produces the output
file (e. g. f.exit). Each task generates output data after it has completed   (f_{12}, f_{13}, f_{14}..., f_{ij}).
The task's children use these data, if any. Three computer sources (PC1, PC2 and PC3)
interconnected with varying bandwidth and having its own servers (S1, S2, S3). Therefore,
the main objective is to assign the workflow tasks to the computer sources so that the total
cost of computation is minimized.

1.6   Problem Formulation

The problem can be formulated to identify a task-resource mapping instance P, such that when calculating the total cost incurred using each compute resource PC, the high cost among all the compute resources is minimized. Let $C_{exe}(P)_j$ be the total cost of all the tasks assigned to a compute resource PC_j. The total cost value is computed by summarizing all the node weights of all tasks assigned to each resource in the mapping M. Let $C_{tx}(P)_j$ be the total access cost between tasks assigned to a compute resource PC_j. The $C_{tx}(P)_j$ is the product of the output file size from task k_1 to task k_2 and the cost of communication from the resource where k_1 is mapped ($P(k_1)$) to another resource where k_2 is mapped ($P(k_2)$). The average cost of communication of unit data between two resources is given by $dP(k_1)$, $dP(k_2)$.

$$C_{exe}(P)_j = \sum_k w_{kj} \qquad \forall P(K) = j \qquad (1.1$$

$$C_{tx}(P)_j = \sum_{k1 \in T}\sum_{k2 \in T} d_{P(k1),P(k2)}e_{k1k2} \forall P(K) = j$$

$$\forall P(k_1) = j \text{ and } P(k_2) \neq j \qquad (1.2$$

$$C_{total}(P)_j = C_{exe}(P)_j + C_{tx}(P)_j \qquad (1.3$$

$$Cost(P) = max(C_{total}(P)_j) \; \forall j \in P \qquad (1.4$$

$$Minimize(Cost(P) \quad \forall P) \qquad (1.5$$

Equation 1.4 implies that all the tasks are not mapped to single compute resource. Initial cost maximization will distribute tasks to all the resources. Subsequent minimization of the overall cost indicates that the total cost is minimal even after initial distribution. For a given instance P, the total cost $C_{total}(P)_j$ for a compute resource PC_j is the sum of execution cost and access cost. When estimating the total cost for all the resources, the largest cost for all the resources is minimized. It indirectly ensures that the tasks are not mapped to a single resource and there will be a distribution of cost among the resources.

1.7   Objectives

Metaheuristic techniques are high-level frameworks which utilize heuristics in order to find solutions to combinatorial optimization problems at a finite computational cost. This kind of problem may be classified as NP-hard, or NP-complete or be a problem for which a polynomial time algorithm is known to exist but is not practical. In general, workflow applications are represented as a directed acyclic graph. In general, the mapping of jobs to the computer sources is an NP-complete problem. The primary objective of this work is to derive the metaheuristic approaches for mapping the tasks to the compute resources such that the total cost of computation is minimized.

1.8   Scheduling with Metaheuristic

In general, it is important to calculate, first up all the average computation cost of all tasks on all the compute resources. This cost can be computed for any application by executing each task of an application on a series of known resources (Bittencourt et al. 2010). As the computation cost is inversely proportional to the computation time, the cost is higher for those resources that complete the task quicker.

The first step is to compute the mapping of all tasks in the workflow, irrespective of their dependencies. This mapping optimizes the overall cost of computing the workflow application. By validating the dependencies between the tasks, the algorithm allocates the "ready" tasks to resources according to the solution provided by meta-heuristic algorithm. Next, the scheduler waits for polling time once all the mapped tasks to resources are dispatched for execution. The ready list is updated based on the number of tasks completed, which will now contain the tasks whose parents have completed execution. Afterwords according to the current network load, the average values for communication between resources are updated.

Next, it is necessary to recompute the mappings using metaheuristic approach when the communication costs would have changed. According to the mappings when remote resource management systems are unable to assign task to resources because of resource unavailability, the recomputation dynamically makes the scheduling and balances other tasks' mappings. Based on the recomputed mappings using meta-heuristic optimization methods, the ready tasks are assigned to the compute resources. The aforesaid steps are repeated until all the tasks in the workflow are scheduled.

Calculate total cost of all tasks in all compute resources by sum of execution cost of tasks at resources and communication cost between resources

Set tasks are nodes

Set edges are communication costs of file transferred between tasks

Compute metaheuristic

    for all "ready" tasks {ti} ∈ T do

        Assign tasks {ti} to resources {pj} according to the solution provided by metaheuristic algorithm.

    End for

    Dispatch all the mapped tasks

    Wait for polling time

    Update the ready task list

    Update the cost of communication between resources according to the current network load

    Compute metheuristic optimization algorithm ({ti})

Until there are unscheduled tasks

Figure 1.3 Pseudocode of the scheduling approach

The scheduling with metaheuristic algorithm dynamically updates the communication costs in every scheduling loop. Based on the current network and resource conditions, it recomputes the task-resource mapping. Thus, it optimizes the cost of computation.

1.9   Task to Resource Encoding

The metaheuristic algorithm starts with random initialization of solutions. In this problem, the solutions are the tasks to be assigned and the dimensions of the solutions are the number of tasks in a workflow. The value assigned to each dimension of a solution is the computing resources indices. Thus the solution represents a mapping of resource to a task. Figure 1.4 shows the solution representation for the workflow shown in Figure 1.2.

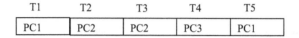

T1	T2	T3	T4	T5
PC1	PC2	PC2	PC3	PC1

Figure 1.4 Solutions representation for the workflow

2. Literature Review

This chapter provides precise elucidation of various works carried out by contemporary researchers on task scheduling problem and various scheduling algorithms for cloud environments based on the metaheuristic techniques. The complexity of the task scheduling problem belongs to NP-complete, involving extremely large search space with a correspondingly large number of potential solutions. In fact, it takes much longer time to find the optimal solution. There is no well-defined methodology to solve the problems under such circumstances.

However in cloud, it is sufficient to find near optimal solution, preferably in a short period of time. In this context IT practioners are focusing on heuristic methods. This chapter focuses on Particle Swarm Optimization (PSO) metaheuristic method of task scheduling used in cloud environment. The objective of the task scheduling problem is to minimize the computation cost.

2.1 Task Scheduling Problem

Cloud computing is a new paradigm for enterprises that can effectively facilitate the execution of tasks. Task scheduling is an important hurdle which is greatly influencing the performance of cloud computing environment. The cloud service provider and clients have different objectives and requirements. In a dynamic environment resource availability and load on resources keep changing from time to time. Therefore, scheduling resources in clouds is a complicated problem.

Scheduling allows optimal allocation of resources among given tasks in a finite time to achieve the desired quality of service. Formally, scheduling problem involves tasks that must be scheduled on resources subject to some constraints to optimize some objective function. The aim is to build a schedule that specifies when and on which resource each task will be executed (Karger et al. 2010). Task scheduling algorithm is a method by which tasks are matched or allocated to data center resources. Generally no perfect task scheduling algorithm exists. A good scheduler implements a suitable compromise or applies a combination of scheduling algorithms according to different applications. A problem can be solved in seconds, hours or even years depending on the algorithm applied. The efficiency of an algorithm is evaluated by the amount of time necessary to execute it. The execution time of an algorithm is stated as a time complexity function relating to the input.

Task Scheduling in Cloud Computing Environment

Tsai et al. (2014) implemented Hyper-Heuristic Scheduling Algorithm (HHSA) for providing effective cloud scheduling solutions. The diversity detection and improvement detection operators are utilized in this approach dynamically to determine better low-level heuristic for the effective scheduling. HHSA can reduce the makespan of task scheduling and improves the overall scheduling performance. The drawback is that the approach has high overhead of connection which reduces the importance of scheduling and thus reduces the overall performance.

Zhu et al. (2014) proffered real-time task oriented Energy Aware (EA) scheduling called EARH for the virtualized clouds. The proposed approach is based on Rolling-Horizon (RH) optimization and the procedures are developed for creation, migration, and cancellation of VMs dynamically to adjust the scale of cloud to achieve real time deadlines

14

and reduce energy. The EARH approach has the drawback of the number of cycles assigned to the VMs that cannot be updated dynamically.

Maguluri & Srikant (2014) suggested a scheduling method for job scheduling with unknown duration in the cloud environment. The job sizes are assumed to be unknown not only at arrival, but also at the beginning of service. Hence the throughput-optimal scheduling and load-balancing algorithm for a cloud data center is introduced, when the job sizes are unknown. This algorithm is based on using queue lengths for weights in max-weight schedule instead of the workload.

Zuo et al. (2014) produced a Self-adaptive Learning Particle Swarm Optimization (SLPSO) based scheduling approach for deadline constraint task scheduling in hybrid Infrastructure as a Service (IaaS) clouds. The approach solves the problem of meeting the peak demand for preserving the quality-of-service constraints by using the PSO optimization technique. The approach provides better scheduling of the tasks by maximizing the profit of IaaS provider while guaranteeing QoS. The problem with this approach is the lack of priority determination which results in failure of deadline tasks. Thus scheduling tasks in a cloud computing environment is a challenging process.

Sahni & Vidyarthi (2015) offered a cost-effective deadline constraint dynamic scheduling algorithm for the scientific workflows. The workflow scheduling algorithms in the grid and clusters are efficient but could not be utilized effectively in the cloud environment because of the on demand resource provisioning and pay-as-you-go pricing model. Hence the scheduling using a dynamic cost-effective deadline-constrained heuristic algorithm has been utilized to exploit the features of cloud by considering the virtual machine performance variability and instance acquisition delay to determine the time scheduling. The problem with the approach is that VMs failures may adversely affect the overall workflow execution time.

Zhu et al. (2015) stipulated an agent-based dynamic scheduling algorithm for effective scheduling of tasks in the virtualized clouds. In this approach, a bidirectional announcement-bidding mechanism and the collaborative process are performed to improve the scheduling performance. To further improve the scheduling, elasticity is considered dynamically to add VMs. The calculation rules are generated to improve the bidding process that in turn reduces the delay. The problem with this approach is that it reduces the performance as it does not consider the communication and dispatching times.

Zhang et al. (2015) put forward a fine-grained scheduling approach called Phase and Resource Information-aware Scheduler for MapReduce (PRISM) for scheduling in the MapReduce model. MapReduce has been utilized for its efficiency in reducing the running time of the data-intensive jobs but most of the MapReduce schedulers are designed on the basis of task-level solutions that provide suboptimal job performance. Moreover, the task-level schedulers face difficulties in reducing the job execution time. Hence the PRISM was developed which divides tasks into phases. Each phase with a constant resource usage profile performs scheduling at the phase level. Thus the overall job execution time can be reduced significantly but the problem of meeting job deadlines in the phase level scheduling is a serious concern that requires specified attention.

Zhu et al. (2016) advanced an Evolutionary Multi-Objective (EMO) workflow scheduling approach to reduce the workflow scheduling problem such as cost and makespan. Due to the specific properties of the workflow scheduling problem, the existing genetic operations, such as binary encoding, real valued encoding and the corresponding variation operators are based on them in the EMO. The problem is that the approach does not consider monetary costs and time overheads of both communication and storage.

2.2 Metaheuristic Methods for Task Scheduling

In computer science and mathematical optimization, metaheuristic is a higher-level procedure or heuristic designed to find, generate, or select a heuristic that may provide a sufficiently good solution to an optimization problem, especially with incomplete or imperfect information or limited computation capacity. Metaheuristics sample a set of solutions which is too large to be completely sampled. Metaheuristics may make a few assumptions about the optimization problem being solved and so they may be usable for a variety of problems. The following sections represent review of Particle Swarm

16

Optimization (PSO) based metaheuristic techniques for workflow scheduling in cloud environment.

Particle swarm optimization based scheduling algorithms

In 1995, Kennedy & Eberhart (1995) introduced an evolutionary computational method, namely Particle Swarm Optimization (PSO) motivated by social behaviour of the particles. Each particle is allied with position and velocity and moves through a multi-dimensional search space. In each iteration, each particle adjusts its velocity based on its best position and the position of the best particle of the whole population. PSO combines local search methods with global search methods by trying to balance exploration and exploitation. PSO has gained popularity due to its simplicity and its usefulness in a broad range of applications with low computational cost.

Tseng et al. (2008) proposed multistage hybrid flow-shop scheduling problem with multiprocessor tasks. They have solved the problem by PSO with a new velocity equation. They have verified the PSO algorithm with nine possible combinations of PSO with three velocity equations and three neighborhood topologies and compared with two existing Genetic Algorithms and an ant colony optimization algorithm.

Pandey et al. (2010) expounded a PSO-based heuristic algorithm for dynamic scheduling of the data intensive workflow applications, where the size and quantity of the data are large. To transfer and store the data as compared to the execution of tasks, more time is needed. This scheme optimizes the cost of the task-resource mapping based on the solution given by the PSO and takes both computation cost and data transmission cost into account.

Guo et al. (2012) formulated a model for task scheduling and mooted a Particle Swarm Optimization (PSO) algorithm which is based on small position value rule to minimize the cost of the processing. By virtue of comparing PSO algorithm with the PSO algorithm embedded in crossover and mutation and in the local research, the experiment results show that the PSO algorithm not only converges faster but also runs faster than the

17

other two algorithms in a large scale. The experiment results prove that the PSO algorithm is more suitable to cloud computing.

Liu & Wang (2012) desihned an algorithm based on PSO to balance the load between virtual machines in cloud. The algorithm tries to minimize makespan and maximize resource utilization of virtual machines. They modified the basic PSO by introducing a self-adapting inertia weight which is based on particle's fitness value and global best fitness value. A simple mutation mechanism is used in which a random value from solution space is assigned to position if there is an overflow.

Yang et al. (2013) recommended a PSO-based algorithm to solve task scheduling and resource allocation in cloud computing. The problem is to assign each subtask to an appropriate resource and to sequence the subtasks on the resources in order to achieve the objectives of this scheme. To formulate the problem, cloud user tasks can denote the set of n independent jobs, and each subtask is allowed to be processed on any given available resources. A subtask is processed on one resource at a time and the given resources are available continuously. This scheme shows that the PSO based fitness function is more effective and efficient with shorter completion time and lower cost.

In this study, the processing cost and makespan associated with the task schedule and the resources allocated are taken into account to measure the performance of the optimization algorithm. The fitness function of this scheme tries to balance the load across the entire system, minimize the makespan and increase the processing capacity. In this scheme, the total completion time serves as the evaluation criterion and includes the total receiving, processing and waiting time of each subtask. The makespan is denoted as the maximum value of the total completion time of each task. Moreover, the total processing capacity on cloud resource is defined as the processing data volume of each unit time.

Huang et al. (2013) set forth a scheme for workflow scheduling to minimize both the total cost and makespan. They present a PSO-based heuristics to realize the optimal mapping for the tunable objective. In this scheme, all the ready tasks assigned to a specific resource are independent, and it will speed up the workflow by scheduling the

18

"bottleneck" task first, i.e. the task having most descendants. Thus, the ready tasks are sorted according to the number of descendants. If there is a tie, the one with a short execution time will be given a high priority to execute first.

3. Improved PSO Algorithm for Workflow Scheduling in Cloud Computing Environments

In the recent years various workflow scheduling approaches have been implemented in order to find the optimum minimal cost. The traditional work flow scheduling techniques deal with statistical approaches. However, Workflow applications are commonly represented as a directed acyclic graph. The mapping of jobs to the computer resources is an NP-complete problem in the general form. Therefore, meta-heuristic approaches have been used for scheduling work- flows. In this chapter, Particle Swarm Optimization (PSO) is discussed and an Improved PSO algorithm for task resource mapping in cloud computing environment with the experimental result analysis is presented.

Swarm Intelligence

Swarm Intelligence (SI) is a computational intelligence technique for solving optimization problems, which are developed from the inspiration of biological examples by flocking, swarming and herding phenomena. The real world problems often are characterized by noisy, incomplete data or multimodality due to their inflexible construction. Conventional computing paradigms show difficulty in optimizing the real world problems. Natural systems have evolved since decades to solve the optimization problems. These natural systems often contain many simple elements that, when working together, produce complex emergent behavior. The natural computing paradigms can be used, where conventional computing paradigm performs unsatisfactorily. Therefore, SI belongs to one such natural computing paradigm.

In general, the biologists have shown great interest in studying collective behavior of social animals such as insects, fish, birds and mammals, since more than five decades.

19

French biologist Pierre-Paul Grasse provided the first ever theoretical explanation of the collective behavior in social insects. In 1984, Grasse (1984) stated the collective behavior of African termites and Craig Reynolds (1987) developed first flocking model in 1987. This was a bio-inspired computational model for simulating the animation of a flock of entities called boid. Deneubourg & Goss (1989), Simon presented collective patterns and decision making in 1989.

In 1991 Deneubourg & Goss (1991) studied the food foraging and the shortest path between the food sources and the nest in ants. At first the term Swarm Intelligence in the context of cellular robotic systems was introduced by Beni and Wang in 1991. In 1992, Marco Dorigo invented Ant Colony Optimization (ACO) algorithm. The ACO is a metaheuristic algorithm that is mimic the food foraging behavior of ants. Particle Swarm Optimization (PSO) is developed by the inspiration of the social behavior of bird flocking or a school of fish, by Eberhart & Kennedy in 1995. In 2005 Artificial Bee Colony (ABC) algorithm was introduced by Karaboga. Basically ABC algorithm simulates the food foraging behavior of honey bees. Nevertheless, the detailed algorithmic explanations of ABC and ACO algorithms are out of scope of the thesis.

Why Swarm Intelligence?

In the natural computing paradigm, Swarm Intelligence (SI) is an emerging research field. It deals with natural and artificial systems composed of many simple individuals. Each of them coordinates using decentralized control and self-organization. It is the outcome of collective behavior of simple individuals that interact with each other and with their environment. It has a great ability to solve complex, multimodal, nondifferentiable, discontinuous and distributed problems. It recommends an optional way to design the systems that are either impossible or near impossible by conventional optimization algorithms. The following properties have been adopted by SI.

- Individuals exchange information directly or via the environment.
- The interactions among the individuals are based on simple behavioral rules.

- It is composed of many simple individuals.
- The individuals are relatively homogeneous.
- The overall behavior of the system results from the interactions of individuals with each other and with their environment.
- Individuals act in a coordinated way without the presence of a coordinator or of an external controller.
- Individuals have the division of labor and distributed task allocation system among them.
- Each individual has a stochastic behavior that depends on its local perception of the neighborhood.

Hence, based on the above properties, SI has maintained a highly important place in computational research domain.

3.1 Particle Swarm Optimization

In 1995, Eberhart & Kennedy (1995) introduced PSO technique. It is a fast, simple and efficient population-based optimization method. PSO is an exciting new methodology in evolutionary computation and a population based optimization tool like Genetic Algorithm (GA). It has been mimicked by the behavior of organisms such as bird flocking and fish schooling. PSO can to run in less computation time and requires less memory because of its inherent simplicity. The basic principle behind the PSO algorithm is that birds find food by flocking but not individually.

This swarm behavior leads to the assumption that information is owned jointly in the flocking. Initially, the swarm has a population which is random solutions. Each potential solution is represented as a particle (agent) and is given a random velocity and is flown through the problem space. Each and every particle has memory and each particle keeps track of its previous best position (p_{best}) and the corresponding fitness value. The swarm has another value called (g_{best}), which is the best value of all particles' p_{best}. It has been shown to be extremely effective in solving a wide range of engineering problems and solves them very quickly.

21

In a PSO, each particle exists in the n-dimensional search space and has certain amount of knowledge. It will move about the search space on the basis of this knowledge. Additionally, the particle has inertia attributed to it and hence will continue to have a component of motion in the direction in which it is moving. The particle knows its location in the search space and will encounter with the best solution. The particle will then modify its direction such that it has additional components towards its own best position (P_{idb}) and towards the overall best position (P_{gdb}).

Since the particle's position in a swarm represents the potential solution, each particle is evaluated based on the fitness function to be optimized. The value of fitness function extrapolates the quality of solution. As the particle flies randomly in D dimensional search space, the position and velocity of ith particle are represented as $X_i = (x_{i1}, x_{i2}, x_{i3}, \cdots, x_{iD})$ and $V_i = (v_{i1}, v_{i2}, v_{i3}, \cdots, v_{iD})$ respectively. In real life applications D refers to the number of variables present in the objective function to be optimized. With increased iteration, particles of the swarm will move towards the global best position by keeping track of their (P_{idb}) and with the influence of (P_{gdb}).

In a D dimensional search space the P_{idb} of the ith particle is represented as $P_{idb} = (p_{i1}, p_{i2}, p_{i3}, \cdots, p_{iD})$ and the P_{gdb} of the whole swarm is represented as $P_{gdb} = (p_1, p_2, p_3, \cdots, p_D)$. The PSO algorithm updates the velocity and position of each particle by the following equations (3.1) and (3.2) respectively.

$$V_{id}^{'} = \omega V_{id} + c_1 rand1()(P_{idb} - X_{id}) + c_2 rand2()(P_{gdb} - X_{id}) \qquad (3.1$$

$$X_{id}^{'} = X_{id} + V_{id}^{'}$$
$$(3.2$$

Where, c_1 and c_2 are the learning factors which determine the relative influence of cognitive and social component respectively. The $rand1()$ and $rand2()$ are uniformly distributed random numbers in the range from 0 to 1. V_{id}, X_{id} and P_{idb} are the velocity, position and the personal best of ith particle in D^{th} dimension. The P_{gdb} is the global best of the swarm in D^{th} dimension.

```
For each particle
   initialize particle
End
Do
   For each particle
   Calculate fitness value
   if the fitness value is better than the best fitness value (P_idb) in history
   set current value as the new P_idb
   end
   choose the particle with the best fitness value of all the particles as the P_gdb
   for each particle
 calculate particle velocity according equation (3.1)
   update particle position according equation (3.2
End
```

Figure 3.1 Pseudocode of the PSO

3.2 Improved Particle Swarm Optimization

In the standard PSO algorithm, the convergence speed of particles is fast, but the adjustments of cognition component and social component make particles search around entire solution. According to velocity and position renewal formula, once the best individual in the swarm is trapped into a local optimum, the information sharing mechanism in PSO will attract other particles to approach this local optimum gradually and in the end, the whole swarm will be converged at this position (Yan et al. 2013). But according to velocity and position renewal equation (3.3) and (3.4), once the whole swarm is trapped into a local optimum, its cognition component and social component will become zero in the end; still, because $0<\omega<1$ and with the increased number of iterations, the velocity of particles will become zero in the end. Thus the whole swarm is hard to jump out of the local optimum if there is no way to achieve the global optimum.

$$V_{id}' = \omega V_{id} + \eta_1 rand()\left(P_{idb} - X_{id}\right) + \eta_2 rand()\left(P_{gdb} - X_{id}\right) \qquad (3.3)$$

$$X_{id}' = X_{id} + V_{id}' \qquad (3.4)$$

Here a fatal weakness may result from this characteristic. With constant increase of iterations, the velocity of particles will gradually diminish and reach zero in the end. At this time, the whole swarm will be converged at one point in the solution space, if P_{gdb} particles haven't found P_{gdb}, the whole swarm will be trapped into a local optimum and the capacity of swarm jump out of a local optimum is rather weak. In order to get through this disadvantage, this work presented a new algorithm based on PSO. In order to avoid being trapped into a local optimum, the new PSO adopts a new information sharing mechanism (Yan et al. 2013). It is known that when a particle is searching in the solution space, it does not know the exact position of the optimum solution (Yan et al. 2013). But one can not only record the best positions an individual particle and the whole swarm have experienced, one can also record the worst positions an individual particle and the whole swarm have experienced. Thus we may make individual particles move in the direction of evading the worst positions an individual particle and the whole flocks have experienced, this will surely enlarge the global searching space of particles and enable them to avoid being trapped into a local optimum too early. At the same time, it will improve the possibility of finding global best in the searching space. In the new strategy, the particle velocity and position renewal formula are as follows:

$$V_{id}' = \omega V_{id} + \eta_1 rand()(X_{id} - P_{idw}) + \eta_2 rand()(X_{id} - P_{gdw})$$

$$(3.5)$$

$$X_{id}' = X_{id} + V_{id}'$$

$$(3.6)$$

Here, P_{idw}, P_{gdw} represent the worst position particle id has found and the worst positions of the whole swarm has found.

In standard PSO algorithm, the next flying direction of each particle is nearly determined; it can fly to the best individual and the best individuals for the whole swarm. In order to decrease the possibility of being trapped into the local optimum, the new PSO introduces genetic selection strategy: To set particle number in the swarm as m, father population and son population add up to $2m$. To select q pairs from m randomly from individual particle i. If the fitness value of i is smaller than its opponents, i will win out and then add one to its mark and finally select those particles which have the maximum

24

mark value into the next generation. The experiments conducted show that this strategy greatly reduces the possibility of being trapped into a local optimum when solving certain functions.

```
For each particle
        Initialize particle
End
do
    for each particle
        calculate fitness value
        if the fitness value is better than the best fitness value (p_idb) in history
    set current value as the new p_idb
    end
    choose the particle with the best fitness value of all the particles as the p_gdb
    for each particle
        calculate particle velocity according equation (3.1) (3.5)
        update particle position according equation (3.2) (3.6)
    end
```

Figure 3.3 Pseudo code of the Improved PSO

4. EXPERIMENTAL RESULTS AND ANALYSIS

Experimental Setup

This research work is experimented and analyzed with the cloudsim used and it consists of 10 resources with different processing speed and hence with different prices, similar to Amazon EC2 services. Due to the nature of metaheuristic algorithm and random initial positions, each algorithm has been implemented 30 times on average and the obtained average results are considered as a final answer and criteria for comparison.

The minimum computation cost value of the best solutions is recorded throughout the optimization of 50 iterations of all tasks completed. The test has been conducted for the task scheduling problem from 10 processors with 100 tasks. In IPSO algorithm, the parameters were set such that the number of particle is 50, the self-recognition coefficient *c1* and social coefficient *c2* are 2 and the weight w is 0.9. The experimental parameter settings of PSO and IPSO algorithms are shown in Table 3.1.

Table 4.1 Parameters and its value for PSO and IPSO

Parameter description	Parameter value
Size of Swarm	50
Self-recognition coefficient *c1*	2
Social coefficient *c2*	2
Weight *w*	0.9
Iterations	50

Experimental Results

Figures 4.1-4.5 plots the convergence of total cost computed by PSO and IPSO over the 50 number of iterations for different sizes of total data processed by the workflow such as 64 MB, 128 MB, 256 MB, 512 MB and 1024 MB respectively. Initially, the particles are randomly initialized. Therefore, the initial total cost is always high. This initial cost corresponds to the 0th iteration. As the algorithm progresses, the convergence is drastic and it finds a global minima very quickly. The average number of iterations needed for the convergence is seen to be 30-35, for this application environment. It displays that IPSO usually had better average completion time values than that of PSO.

Figure 4.1 shows the computation cost of PSO and IPSO scheduling algorithm for 64 MB. For IPSO, the number of iterations needed for the convergence is seen to be 40. It shows IPSO usually spent the shorter time to complete the scheduling than PSO algorithm. It is to be noted that IPSO usually spent the shorter time to accomplish the various scheduling tasks and had the better result compared with PSO algorithm.

26

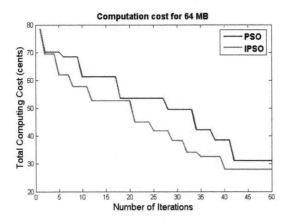

Figure 4.1 Performance of PSO and IPSO scheduling algorithm for 64 MB

Figure 4.2 shows the computation cost of PSO and IPSO scheduling algorithm for 128 MB. For IPSO, the number of iterations needed for the convergence is seen to be 36.

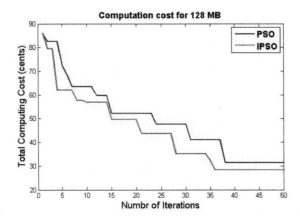

Figure 4.2 Performance of PSO and IPSO scheduling algorithm for 128 MB

Figure 4.3 shows the computation cost of PSO and IPSO scheduling algorithm for 256 MB. For IPSO, the number of iterations needed for the convergence is seen to be 40.

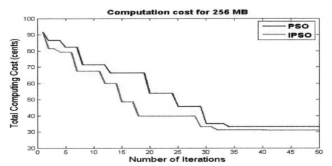

Figure 4.3 Performance of PSO and IPSO scheduling algorithm for 256 MB

Figure 4.4 shows the computation cost of PSO and IPSO scheduling algorithm for 512 MB. For IPSO, the number of iterations needed for the convergence is seen to be 35.

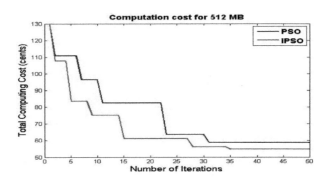

Figure 4.4 Performance of PSO and IPSO scheduling algorithm for 512 MB

Figure 4.5 shows the computation cost of PSO and IPSO scheduling algorithm for 1024 MB. For IPSO, the number of iterations needed for the convergence is seen to be 22.

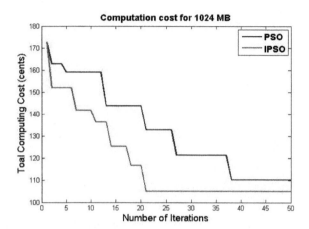

Figure 4.5 Performance of PSO and IPSO scheduling algorithm for 1024 MB

Table 4.2 plots comparison of optimal total cost between PSO based resource selection and IPSO algorithms when varying total data size of a workflow. IPSO achieves 10.19 percentages of improvements for 64 MB of total data processed than the PSO algorithm. For 128 MB and 512 MB, the proposed IPSO method attains 9.89 and 6.83 percentage of improvements respectively. For 1024 MB the proposed IPSO method returns 4.83 percentage of improvements in optimal total computation cost. Clearly, IPSO based mapping has much lower cost as compared to that of the existing PSO based mapping. In addition, the slope of the trend line of all the figures shows that PSO based mapping reduces the cost linearly, whereas the IPSO reduces exponentially and maintains a balanced the intensification and diversification in the entire search space.

Table 4.2 Comparison of optimal minimum cost of computation with various data size for PSO and IPSO

Size of Data	PSO	IPSO	Percentage of Improvement
64 MB	31.19	28.01	10.19%
128 MB	31.32	28.22	9.89%
256 MB	33.03	30.96	6.26%
512 MB	58.7	54.69	6.83%
1024 MB	110.4	105.06	4.83%

5. Conclusion

The IPSO algorithm for workflow scheduling is capable of overcoming the poor convergence problem of PSO method. It focuses on mapping task and resource with minimum computation cost. In the IPSO method the worst positions of the individual particle are recorded and applied in the whole swarm. Thus it may make individual particles move in the direction of evading the worst positions of the individual particle and of the whole flock. This will surely enlarge the global searching space of particles and enable them to avoid being trapped into a local optimum too early. The result of total cost of execution was obtained by varying the data size and is plotted in various figures and also comparison is made with IPSO against PSO. It is found that IPSO based task-resource mapping can achieve better cost savings when compared to PSO based mapping for application workflow.

5. References

1. Beni, G & Wang, J, 1991, 'Theoretical problems for the realization of distributed robotic system', Proceedings of IEEE International Conference on Robotics and Automation, pp. 1914 – 1920.

2. Bittencourt, LF, Sakellariou, R & Madeira, RM, 2010, 'DAG Scheduling Using a Look ahead Variant of the Heterogeneous Earliest Finish Time Algorithm', Proceedings of 2010 18th Euromicro conference on Parallel, Distributed and Network-based Processing, pp. 27-34.

3. Blum, C & Roli, A, 2003, 'Metaheuristics in combinatorial optimization: Overview and conceptual comparison', Journal of ACM Computing Surveys, vol. 35, no. 3, pp. 268-308.

4. Campos, M, Krohling, R & Enriquez, I, 2014, 'Bare Bones Particle Swarm Optimization With Scale Matrix Adaptation', IEEE Transactions on Cybernetics, vol. 44, no. 9, pp. 1567-1578.

5. Chen, WN & Zhang, J, 2009, 'An ant colony optimization approach to a grid workflow scheduling problem with various QoS requirements', IEEE Transactions on Systems, Man, and Cybernetics, vol. 39, no. 1, pp. 29–43.

6. Deneubourg, JL & Goss, S, 1989, 'Collective patterns and decision making', Ethology, Ecology and Evolution, vol. 1, no. 4, pp. 295–311.

7. Deneubourg, JL, Goss, S, Franks, N, Franks, AS, Detrain, C & Chretien, L, 1990, 'The dynamics of collective sorting robot-like ants and ant-like robots', Proceedings of the first international conference on simulation of adaptive behavior on from animals to animats, pp. 356–363.

8. Eberhart, R & Kenedy, J, 1995, 'A new optimizer using particle swarm theory', Proceedings of Sixth International Symposium on Micro Machine and Human Science, pp. 39–43.

9. Eberhart, R & Kenedy, J, 1995, 'Particle swarm optimization', Proceedings of IEEE International Conference on Neural Networks, pp. 1114–1121.

10. Fesanghary, M, Damangir, E & Soleimani, I, 2009, 'Design optimization of shell and tube heat exchangers using global sensitivity analysis and harmony search algorithm', Applied Thermal Engineering, vol. 29, no. 6, pp. 1026–1031.

11. Glover, F, 1986, 'Future Paths for Integer Programming and Links to Artificial

Intelligence', Computers and Operations Research, vol. 13, no. 5, pp. 533-549.

12. Grasse, PH, 1984, Termitologia, Tome II. Fondation des Societs. Paris, Masson.

13. Guo, L, Zhao, S, Shen, S & Jiang, C, 2012, 'Task Scheduling Optimization in Cloud Computing Based on Heuristic Algorithm', Journal of Networks, vol. 7, no. 3, pp. 547-553.

14. He, HD, Lu, WZ & Xue, Y, 2014, 'Prediction of particulate matter at street level using artificial neural networks coupling with chaotic particle swarm optimization algorithm', Building and Environment, vol. 78, no. 8, pp. 111–117.

15. Huang, J, Wu, K, Leong, LK, Ma, S & Moh, M, 2013, ' A tunable workflow scheduling algorithm based on particle swarm optimization for cloud computing', The International Journal of Soft Computing and Software Engineering, vol. 3, no. 3, pp. 351-358.

16. Jamalipour, M, Sayareh, R, Gharib, M, Khoshahval, F & Karimi MR, 2013, 'Quantum behaved Particle Swarm Optimization with Differential Mutation operator applied to WWER-1000 in-core fuel management optimization', Annals of Nuclear Energy, vol. 54, no. 4, pp. 134–140.

17. Jau, YM, Su ,KL, Wu ,CJ & Jeng, JT, 2013, 'Modified quantum-behaved particle swarm optimization for parameters estimation of generalized nonlinear multi-regressions model based on Choquet integral with outliers', Applied Mathematics and Computation, vol. 221, no. 9, pp. 282–295.

18. Karger, D, Stein, C & Wein, J, 2010, 'Scheduling Algorithms. Algorithms and theory of computation handbook', Special topics and techniques, CRC Press, Florida, United States.

19. Kashan, AH & Karimi, B, 2009, 'A discrete particle swarm optimization for scheduling parallel machines', Computers and Industrial Engineering, vol. 59, no. 1, pp. 216-223.

20. Kaveh, A & Talatahari, S, 2009, 'Engineering Optimization with Hybrid Particle Swarm and Ant Colony Optimization', Asian Journal of Civil Engineering Building and Housing, vol. 10, no. 6, pp. 611-628.

21. Kennedy, J & Eberhart, R, 1995, 'Particle swarm optimization', Proceedings of IEEE International Conference on Neural Networks, pp.1942-1948.

22. Li ,CS, Zhou, J, Kou, P & Xiao J, 2012, 'A novel chaotic particle swarm optimization based fuzzy clustering algorithm', Neuro computing, vol. 83, no. 4, pp. 98–109.

23. Li, P & Xiao, H, 2014, 'An improved quantum-behaved particle swarm optimization algorithm', Applied Intelligence, vol. 40, no. 3, pp. 479–496.

24. Liu, B, Wang, L & Jin, YH, 2008, 'An effective hybrid PSO-based algorithm for flow, shop scheduling with limited buffers', Computers and Operations Research, vol. 35, no. 9, pp. 2791-2806.

25. Liu, Z, & Wang X, 2012, 'A PSO-based algorithm for load balancing in virtual machines of cloud computing environment', Proceedings of the Third international conference on Advances in Swarm Intelligence, pp. 142-147.

26. Maguluri, ST & Srikant, R, 2014, 'Scheduling jobs with unknown duration in clouds', IEEE/ACM Transactions on Networking, vol. 22, no. 6, pp. 1938–1951.

27. Manvi, SS & Shyam, GK, 2014, 'Resource management for Infrastructure as a Service (IaaS) in cloud computing: A survey', Journal of Network and Computer Applications, vol. 41, no. 5, pp. 424–440.

28. Moraga, R, DePuy, G & Whitehouse, G, 2006, Metaheuristics: A solution methodology for optimization problems: Handbook of Industrial and Systems Engineering, CRC Press, Florida, United States.

29. Pandey, S, Wu, L, Guru, SM, & Buyya, R, 2010, 'A Particle Swarm Optimization-based Heuristic for Scheduling Workflow Applications in Cloud Computing Environments', Proceedings of 2010 24th IEEE International Conference on Advanced Information Networking and Applications, pp. 400-40.

30. Qin, X, Yang, Z, Li, W & Yang, Y, 2013, 'Optimized task scheduling and resource allocation in cloud computing using PSO based fitness function', Information Technology Journal, vol. 12, no. 23, pp. 7090–7095.

31. Reynolds, CW, Flocks & Herds, 1987,'A distributed behavioral model', Proceedings of 14th Annual Conference on Computer Graphics and Interactive Techniques SIGGRAPH'87, pp. 25–34.

32. Rodrigues, D, Pereira, L, Almeida, T, Papa, J, Souza, A, Ramos, C & Yang, XS, 2013, 'BCS: A binary cuckoo search algorithm for feature selection', Proceeding of IEEE International Symposium on Circuits and Systems, pp. 465–468.

33. Sahni, J & Vidyarthi, D, 2015, 'A Cost-effective Deadline-constrained Dynamic Scheduling Algorithm for scientific workflows in a cloud environment', IEEE Transactions on Cloud Computing, vol.4, no.1, pp. 5065-5082.

34. Talia, D, 2013, 'Workflow Systems for Science: Concepts and Tools', ISRN Software Engineering, vol. 3, no. 12, pp. 1-15.

35. Tasgetiren, MF, Liang, YC, Sevkli, M & Gencyilmaz, G, 2007, 'A particle swarm optimization algorithm for make span and total flow time minimization in the permutation

flowshop sequencing problem', European Journal of Operational Research, vol. 177, no. 3, pp.1930-1947.

36. Torabi, SA, Sahebjamnia, N, Mansouri, SA & Bajestani, MA, 2013, 'A particle swarm optimization for a fuzzy multi-objective unrelated parallel machines scheduling problem', Applied Soft Computing, vol. 13, no. 12, pp. 4750-4762.

37. Tsai, WC, Huang, WC, Chiang, MH, Chiang, MC & Yang, CS, 2014, 'A hyper-heuristic scheduling algorithm for cloud', IEEE Transactions on Cloud Computing, vol. 2, no. 2, pp. 236–250.

38. Tseng, CT & Liao, CJ, 2008, 'A particle swarm optimization algorithm for hybrid flow-shop scheduling with multiprocessor tasks', International Journal of Production Research, vol. 46, no. 17, pp. 4655-4670.

39. Voss, S, 2001, Meta-heuristics: The state of the art: Local Search for Planning and Scheduling, Lecture Notes on Artificial Intelligence, 2148, pp. 1-23.

40. Zeng, YJ & Sun, YG, 2014, 'An improved particle swarm optimization for the combined heat and power dynamic economic dispatch problem', Electric Power Components and Systems, vol. 42, no. 15, pp. 1700–1716.

41. Pandey, S., Wu, L., Guru, S.M., & Buyya, R.,2010, ' A particle swarm optimization-based heuristic for scheduling workflow applications in cloud computing environments', In Advanced Information Networking and Applications ,24th IEEE International Conference, pp.400-407.

42. Zhang, H, Fernández, JA, Rangaiah GP, Petriciolet, AB & Segovia, JG ,2011, 'Evaluation of integrated differential evolution and unified bare-bones particle swarm optimization for phase equilibrium and stability problems', Fluid Phase Equilibria, vol. 310, no. 2, pp. 129–141.

43. Zhang, H, Kennedy, DD, Rangaiah, GP & Petriciolet, AB, 2011, 'Novel bare-bones particle swarm optimization and its performance for modeling vapor-liquid equilibrium data', Fluid Phase Equilibria, vol. 301, no. 1, pp. 33–45.

44. Zhang, Q, Zhani, MF, Yang, Y, Boutaba, R & Wong, R, 2015, 'PRISM: fine-grained resource-aware scheduling for MapReduce', IEEE Transactions on Cloud Computing, vol. 3, no. 2, pp. 182–194.

45. Zhang, Y & Wu, L, 2011, 'Crop classification by forward neural network with adaptive chaotic particle swarm optimization', Sensors, vol. 11, no. 5, pp. 4721–4743.

46. Zhu, X, Yang, LT, Chen, H, Wang, J, Yin, S & Liu, X, 2014, 'Realtime tasks oriented energy-aware scheduling in virtualized clouds', IEEE Transactions on Cloud Computing,

vol. 2, no. 2, pp. 168–180.

47. Zhu, Z, Chen, C, Yang, LT & Xiang, Y, 2015, 'ANGEL: agent based scheduling for real-time tasks in virtualized clouds', IEEE Transactions on Computers, vol. 64, no. 12, pp. 3389–340.

48. Zhu, Z, Zhang, G, Li, M & Liu, X, 2016, 'Evolutionary Multi-objective workflow scheduling in cloud', IEEE Transactions on Parallel and Distributed Systems, vol. 27, no. 5, pp. 1344–1357.

49. Zuo, X, Zhang, G & Tan, W, 2014, 'Self-adaptive learning PSO based deadline constrained task scheduling for hybrid IaaS cloud', IEEE Transactions on Automation Science and Engineering, vol. 11, no. 2, pp. 564–573.

ISBN 978-3-96067-192-3

9 783960 671923

Anchor Academic Publishing
Hermannstal 119k
22119 Hamburg

www.anchor-publishing.com